The Brain Accelerator

Rock the SAT and ACT

With Revolutionary Techniques

Tom Luna

ISBN: 978-1-329-01478-7

To my parents, Bob and June Luna

Thank you for all of your love, patience, and encouragement

To my wife, Jennifer

All my love and thanks for putting up with me

To my kids, Brittany, Tyler, Brooke, and now Joey

I love you all

Table of Contents

Table of Contents

What's a Little Mass Hysteria Among Friends?

"You tutored my son, McKay, in math last spring before the SAT. His score did go up (can't remember how much at the moment, but it was what you said to expect). Thank you for your help. You also deserve thanks, because McKay applied for early admission to the University of Georgia (the only place he wants to go), and HE GOT IN!!! He found out Friday. Teenage boys do holler, jump up and down, and don't mind when their moms cry in these situations! It was fabulous." (an email received from a former student's very happy mom)

Why did I write this book? I could list many reasons for writing this book. One could be that my wife of 32 years has been suggesting (nagging?) for many years that I should do it. If you've been married for any length of time, you know that it's usually (always?) a good idea to do what your wife keeps suggesting (over and over).

Another reason I could list is that I want to leave some sort of legacy for my three kids. I suppose this is true. I love my kids, and it would be nice to believe that my kids think well of me and would brag about me to the grandkids. However, my kids know I love them, and hopefully we've made enough great memories together, I've performed enough "dad miracles" (you know, something that only dad can do, and he comes through), and made them laugh often enough that they'll brag on me to the grandkids without having to go through the agony and ecstasy of writing this book.

I could list other reasons, too, but the real reason I wrote this book was so that more moms, dads, sons, and daughters could have an experience like the above family had. Having a role in an experience like that is priceless. It transcends. It uplifts. It magnifies your existence.

My wife has been an Emergency Room and Intensive Care Registered Nurse for over 30 years. I can't count the number of times that she has come home and shared an experience from her day describing how she has brought comfort to a family or patient dealing with great distress or loss, averted disaster by taking some timely action, or literally snatching a patient's life back from the jaws of death. To these families and patients she is an angel sent from God. She is their own personal miracle walking on two legs. I can only aspire to that kind of service.

While I doubt the information and advice contained in this book will likely ever save someone's life, I know that it can change many, many lives for the better. It can help sons and daughters be the first in their families to get a college education. It can help sons and daughters get a better education by going to better schools. It can help moms and dads pay for this increasingly more expensive education by enabling the sons and daughters to qualify for scholarships – scholarships that make affordable that which would be unaffordable. And when these sons and daughters have sons and daughters, maybe, just maybe, they'll be able to pass a legacy on to the next generation. Then they can jump up and down and cry, too.

That's why I wrote this book.

I Didn't Expect the Spanish Inquisition!

Hundreds of times parents have told me, "My son/daughter gets good grades, but then they do lousy on these tests!" Sound familiar? Have you said that yourself? Why is that? Why does a successful student in school have so much trouble when it comes to taking the SAT or ACT tests?

It happens for several reasons. First, there is the truism that being able to FIND information is not the same as KNOWING it. Homework, open book tests, projects, etc. allow you to FIND information and build a grade, but a test, for the most part, requires you to KNOW the information. It must be stored in the data banks of your brain, and then you must be able to retrieve it. That's not always easy to do, especially under time pressure. The techniques outlined in this book will make this process much easier by teaching you how to more fully utilize the capabilities of your brain and score much higher. These techniques will ACCELERATE your brain!

Another reason this happens is that these tests are structured much differently than any test in your school. The tests in school are limited in scope, only covering a chapter or at most one year's worth of material. The SAT and ACT cover everything you've learned (or haven't learned) in your life! In the education biz, that is what is referred to as "comprehensive." Us common folk call it A HELLUVA LOT!

In addition, the questions themselves are constructed in a much more complex manner. A typical Math question in a high school algebra class will usually look something like this:

Solve for x: $x/4 - x/6 = 3$

Now look at a similar question that was taken from an SAT practice test:

Let "$a\Omega$" be defined for all positive integers "a" by the equation "$a\Omega$" = $a/4 - a/6$. If "$x\Omega$" = 3, what is the value of "x"?

In both cases, the answer is 36, but where did "$a\Omega$" come from, and what does that have to do with the solution? It reminds me of this old grade school joke, "What is gray, has big ears, four legs, a trunk, and drives a pick-up truck? The answer is an elephant. The driving part was just to make it harder!"

Take heart, though, because there is another difference between high school tests and the SAT and ACT tests, and that is the scale. High school tests generally require at least 70% correct to barely obtain a "C" grade. A "C" means you are mediocre, but you are passing. Not many colleges will be excited about recruiting a "C" student, unless, of course, that student can run a 40 – yard dash in 4.4 seconds or dunk a basketball with his teeth! However, if a student gets a 70% correct on the SAT Math, their score is 600, and 70% correct on the ACT Math scores a 26. Both scores are considerably higher than average and would enable most students to attend all but the more selective schools.

This book is designed to help you achieve a significantly higher score on the SAT and ACT tests. It is that simple. It is not designed to help you read or write any better, although that may be a byproduct. It is not designed to help you understand or enjoy Math more fully, although that, too, may happen.

"But," you may ask, "aren't those worthy goals, and shouldn't they be addressed?" Yes, they are, and, yes, they should. It just isn't the goal of this book. "Well, why not?" Because the universities that use the SAT and ACT scores to decide whether or not to admit you and the organizations that use these scores to decide whether or not to award a scholarship to you do not care how the you achieved that score (as long as no cheating was involved, of course). They merely look at a number. They will not ask what kind of preparation helped you score higher than the students that they turned away or to which they denied a scholarship.

When I was playing baseball at the University of Nevada, Las Vegas, in the early eighties, we played as an independent with no conference affiliation. As such, we had to qualify for the NCAA College World Series playoffs by winning enough games, usually 40 or more, during the regular season to be awarded an at-large berth. We had no way to automatically qualify by winning the most games in our conference or winning a conference tournament as other teams did. We were judged solely on the basis of how many total games we won.

Given this situation, we adopted this saying as our mantra, "They don't ask how. They just ask how many!" This crystallized our focus on winning games. It didn't matter if we won by ten runs or one run. It didn't matter if we won by superior pitching, hitting, or defense. It didn't matter if we won by dumb luck! There was no such thing as a moral victory. A win was a win, and a loss wasn't good enough. Both years I played there, we went to the playoffs. Many goals can be achieved if your focus is clear.

So it is, also, with taking the SAT and ACT tests. Your focus must be to score as high as possible on the test. That is the objective, pure and simple. Any other goal is secondary, and, quite frankly, not worth considering within this context.

Now, make no mistake, there is no moral/legal way to "cheat" the SAT or ACT. I do not encourage nor condone such attempts. That's NOT what this book is about.

There is also no substitute for knowing the subject material. You should still know by now the differences and uses of a comma and a semi-colon, a rectangle and a trapezoid, and a variable and a constant.

This book will give you helpful hints and keys to understanding and quickly analyzing the questions on the subject matter. More importantly, however, this book will outline for you revolutionary techniques to use when taking the SAT or ACT that maximizes your brain utilization and scoring potential. These techniques ACCELERATE your brain. While the techniques described will take some practice to become most effective, they are simple enough that anyone can learn and utilize them. These techniques were developed over many years, and they are supported by scientific research conducted by experts in the field of Neuroscience studying the optimal functioning of the brain with respect to learning, memory, and recall.

There is nothing complicated in these techniques, but they are extremely powerful. I have had students increase their scores by as much as 55% literally from one test to the next. The average increase has been about 20% on the SAT and 25% on the ACT. This is HUGE, especially when ten points on the SAT or one point on the ACT can make the difference between success and failure when it comes to admission to school or receiving a scholarship.

The College Board (developer and owner of the SAT) maintains that the SAT test is essentially uncoachable, and research by the College Board and the National Association of College Admission Counseling suggest that tutoring courses result in an average increase of about 20 points on the Math section and 10 points on the verbal section (less than half of 1%). Other studies by Ohio State University and University of Oxford found that SAT prep/coaching courses boosted scores an average 56 – 60 points. That would be an increase in the 2.5% to 4% range, depending on the previous score.

Why am I getting increases averaging 20% - 25% (with some exceeding 50%) when other formal programs average at best 4%? Because the techniques contained in this book deal with maximizing scores based on what your brain can do, rather than trying to exploit a specific weakness, flaw, or characteristic in either test. While the SAT and ACT use different methods and philosophies, these BRAIN ACCELERATOR techniques are equally applicable to either test, because the brain works the same!

Oh, What a Tangled Web We Weave!

The SAT (originally Scholastic Aptitude Test) and ACT (originally American College Test) were designed to assist universities and colleges in the identification of suitable candidates for admission. The tests have tried to predict who is "college ready" and at what level, since the more selective schools are looking for the top students.

The SAT was created in 1926 and served about a dozen colleges. The ACT was first administered in 1959 as a competitor to the SAT. Today over 80% of the 4-year schools in the United States require an SAT or ACT score for admission consideration, and many more use the scores in the admission evaluation process, although it is not required.

Why do so many schools rely on these tests so heavily over other criteria like grade point average? Two reasons, really. First, grades achieved in one high school are not necessarily comparable to those achieved in another high school. Sometimes it varies from teacher to teacher within the same school. We all remember being warned about who the

13

"tough" teachers were. Well, if the value of a grade can vary from teacher to teacher, imagine how the grades might vary from one school to another in different parts of the country! A national, arbitrary measuring stick is preferable in order to accurately gauge a student's capability.

Second, school admissions officials and those who make decisions at scholarship organizations use these scores to quickly and arbitrarily cull the "cream of the crop" from the thousands of applications they receive every year. This makes their job easier. In addition, supply and demand affects their decisions. When the demands for admissions or scholarships rise in relation to the supply, they can easily raise the criteria. When the demand/supply ratio falls, they can easily lower the criteria. Also, objective (quantifiable) criteria, like a test score, are more easily defended rather than subjective (opinion oriented) criteria, like evaluating an essay. In the end, easy wins out.

While the goals and uses of the SAT and ACT are pretty much the same, their philosophy and methods are different. They are created differently and scored differently (see Table I for a comparative guide to the two scoring systems), although the end result of a quantifiable score/ranking is achieved.

The primary difference between the two tests hinges on the philosophy under which they were created and have evolved. The ACT strives to be an all-encompassing "final exam" covering material that should have been learned in high school or before. The questions tend to be relatively straightforward (like high school), and the test covers more subjects than the SAT (Science and Trigonometry, for instance).

The SAT has historically endeavored to determine a student's "innate ability," probably arising from the fact that the original test was derived from a World War I Army I.Q. test. As such, the SAT uses more ambiguously phrased, "tricky" questions that require more analytical skills than the ACT. In short, you must figure out what the question is REALLY asking before you can go about answering it. The difficulty of the ACT comes from the breadth of the material covered, the volume covered, fewer breaks allowed between sections, and less time allotted per question in relation to the SAT. The

15

Table I

Estimated Relationship: SAT Combined Score/ACT Composite Score

SAT Score (Single Score) Reading+Math+Writing	SAT Score (Range) Reading+Math+Writing	ACT Composite Score
2390	2380 – 2400	36
2330	2290 – 2370	35
2250	2220 – 2280	34
2180	2140 – 2210	33
2120	2080 – 2130	32
2060	2020 – 2070	31
2000	1980 – 2010	30
1940	1920 – 1970	29
1880	1860 – 1910	28
1820	1800 – 1850	27
1770	1740 – 1790	26
1710	1680 – 1730	25
1650	1620 – 1670	24
1590	1560 – 1610	23
1530	1510 – 1550	22
1470	1450 – 1500	21
1410	1390 – 1440	20
1350	1330 – 1380	19
1290	1270 – 1320	18
1230	1210 – 1260	17

difficulty of the SAT comes from its use of intentionally confusing wording, similar answers, the need for comparative analysis (especially in the Reading section), and the time pressure created by these devices.

In addition, the SAT penalizes a student for any wrong answer on any of the multiple choice questions (the ACT does not). This is supposed to discourage "guessing" on the test by establishing a penalty for guessing wrong. What it really does is add another layer of analysis to determine the expected value (thus further squeezing the time) of answering a question (versus leaving it unanswered) rather than encouraging "first impression" or "innate knowledge" type answers.

Over the last 20 years, and especially the last 10 years, the SAT has encountered severe criticism from educators, students, and admissions officials for its methods and results. Educators and students have long complained that it doesn't reflect the educational experience of the student, and admissions officials have noted that grade point average, rather than the SAT score, has been a better predictor of college success.

Another complaint about the SAT has been the capricious (now there's a good SAT essay word!) nature of the essay portion of the test and the lack of cogent (aha! another good essay word!) standards by which the essay is graded. For as long as the essay has been a part of the test, adroit (wow! I'm on a roll now!) essay writers have known that the key to high essay scores lies in the use of esoteric (hey! this would make a great essay!) words and voluminous (I rest my case) amounts of writing. In other words, make it fancy, and make it long. Accuracy of facts or dates is unnecessary. In fact, the graders are not allowed to downgrade an essay for inaccuracies.

Dr. Les Perelman, Director of Undergraduate Writing at the Massachusetts Institute of Technology, has long been a critic of the test's essay portion. He has long objected to the nature of the essay question – that is, asking students to write thoughtfully on a subject that they have never thought about previously. Oh yes, and please do it in a limited amount of time. He also found a direct correlation between the length of the essay and the score. He found that the longer the essay was, the higher the score it received. It was so obvious to him that he found he could correctly predict the score an essay would receive simply by looking at it without reading it.

This doubt about and dislike of the SAT has led to two results. First, in 2011 the ACT had more total test takers than the SAT for the first time in its history. Second, the SAT is undergoing a major overhaul. The intent of this overhaul is to become more straightforward, more high school curriculum oriented, more predictive of college success – essentially, more like the ACT. These changes are due to be rolled out with the test in March of 2016.

Many students have asked me, "Which test should I take?" My answer is always, "It depends." If the student considers themselves to be a good test taker, analytical thinker, or Science (and to a much lesser degree Trigonometry) tends to be a problem subject, then the SAT is probably the better choice. If the opposite is true, then the ACT is probably better. I usually encourage the student to take both tests, especially if they have taken only one or none of them. This way they get a better feel for which one bests suits their skills and temperament.

The wonderful thing is that the information and techniques described later in the book will help immensely on either test. They are not test specific (with a couple exceptions that are noted). In fact, the techniques will not even be affected by the changes coming on the SAT, so they are not time sensitive or heading towards obsolescence. These techniques work with your brain to optimize the use of your brain. The brain is the constant in this scenario, so we are going to ACCELERATE IT!

Eat Until It's Coming Out Both Ears!

All right, then. Now that we understand the problem, let's start talking about the solution. Besides understanding the subject material, which you have hopefully acquired during your schooling or through additional review, there are two things that will turbo-charge your progress toward the score you desire. The first I call **Magic Nuggets**. The second I call **The Brain Accelerator**. If **The Brain Accelerator** is the main course, then **Magic Nuggets** are definitely the appetizer, soup, and salad! As in any great meal, they compliment each other and create a complete, satisfying experience.

Magic Nuggets are just that: little nuggets made up of hints, keys, and shortcuts that work like magic. They create a faster way to answer a problem correctly, and make no mistake, faster is better! Time is the enemy on these tests. It is the vulture perched on your shoulder waiting to snatch your testing life away from you, and these **Magic Nuggets** keep that vulture at bay.

The **Magic Nuggets** are helpful in all areas of the test. Some are big, all encompassing keys, and some are small hints that make a problem simpler or keep you out of a trap. Some of these **Magic Nuggets** you might find in a good study guide, but most of them you won't. They go beyond the study guides.

You will find that most of the **Magic Nuggets** deal with the Math section. There are **Magic Nuggets** for all of the sections, but the Math section is the most diverse. It covers basic Arithmetic, basic Algebra, advanced Algebra, Data Analysis, Statistics, Plane and Coordinate Geometry, and in the case of the ACT, Trigonometry. The majority of students have the most trouble with the Math section, so that is where I will give the most **Magic Nuggets**.

The Brain Accelerator is a series of techniques that really puts this process into hyperdrive! The techniques are easy to learn, but they are EXTREMELY powerful and backed up by scientific research from some of the best minds in the field of Neuroscience. More on that later!

You'll Know 'Em When You See 'Em!

Magic Nuggets - Writing/English

The Writing (SAT) or English (ACT) section is made up of various parts depending on which test you take. Both contain multiple choice questions designed to test grammar, sentence structure, and punctuation. The SAT also includes a mandatory written essay, although, like the current ACT, the SAT will convert to an optional essay with the new test revisions in 2016. Optional or not, some universities require an essay to be done with the test, so check the requirements of whatever school it is in which you may be interested.

The use and meanings of many words in the English language have changed over the years. Many words, like pot, text, pin, and tweet, have either changed or added new meanings. However, the rules of grammar, sentence structure, and punctuation have not changed, and the writers of these tests must conform to them. For instance, the preceding sentence used four commas. The first was used to create a pause emphasizing a contrast from the previous thought, the middle two separated members of a list, and the fourth was used with a conjunction (and) joining two complete sentences. The use of these commas is non-negotiable. The rules are the rules.

Given this fact, it is important to know the rules as much as possible. The nice thing is that the rules don't change. This is unlike the "rules" for spelling, which seem to be more like wishy-washy suggestions. Take for example the rule, "I before E, except after C, or when sounding like A, as in neighbor or weigh." If that didn't include enough exceptions, what do we do with words like science, species, seize, and foreign? Luckily, neither the SAT nor ACT test for spelling!

Anyway, it's easy to find a book or something online that will give you the rules for grammar, sentence structure, and punctuation, and if you learn them all, you'll do just fine. However, that's usually not necessary. I'm going to give you some **Magic Nuggets** that will help.

Improving and Completing Sentences

On both the SAT and ACT, improving sentences takes the form of an underlined set of words in a sentence. Sometimes it is the entire sentence. One of your options is always that the sentence needs no change. Since the SAT gives five possible answers and the ACT gives four, the statistical probability that the correct answer is that the sentence needs no change is 20% and 25%, respectively. That's not a majority of the time, but it (**Magic Nugget**) is significant enough that you should not be afraid to put that as answer. Don't feel that "it must be a trick."

The next **Magic Nugget** is that it is important to understand that there is only one right answer. There may be other answers that could be forced to work, but there is only one that fits like a glove, and the distinction usually hinges on the words used around the word or phrase in question. For example, take a look at the following question.

The judge told the man, "You are _____!"

A) pretty

B) sick

C) guilty

D) amazing

Are all of these answers possible? I suppose, but since a "judge" is speaking, "guilty" is the indicated answer.

Here's one that's a little less obvious, but the answer still hinges on the context.

Looking back on his life, George _____ some of his worst decisions.

A) remembered

B) regretted

C) recanted

D) reviled

While all of these words seem that they could possibly be used, there is only one right answer: regretted. The key here is that George (alone) is looking back at his "worst" decisions. "Remembered" is not strong enough. "Recanted" is something done in public or to another person, but George seems to be alone. "Reviled" means to speak about someone or something in a critical, insulting, or abusive manner, but there is no indication that George goes that far. "Regretted" fits best.

Finding the Error

Finding the error involves grammar, sentence structure, and punctuation, but the primary culprit is sentence structure and the words used within that structure. All sentences must contain a subject (noun or pronoun) and an action or state-of-being (verb). That's it. "Joe ran" is a complete sentence, but almost all sentences contain more than two words. Those other words have to agree with the subject and action words, and, of course, they have to agree with each other. "Ball" and "said" are good subject and action words, but they don't agree with each other. Similarly, "The dog ran together" doesn't work either.

So what makes words "agree?" The primary considerations come down to the next **Magic Nugget**, "How many tents make sense?" "How many" refers to singular (alone) or plural (two or more), "tents" refers to past tense, present tense, and future tense, and "makes sense" refers to whether or not the words used make sense together in the context in which they are written.

Singular or plural subjects must be paired with other singular or plural words. A party is fun, and parties are fun. A party are fun, and parties is fun just doesn't work. The **Magic Nugget** here is the "s" on the end. The "s" on the verb goes with the singular. An army marches, and soldiers march. If it is singular, use the "s"!

Tense tells when something happens, and it must agree with the context. For instance, "The garbage man collected (past tense) the garbage next (future tense) Tuesday" doesn't agree. Similarly, "I will (future tense) do my homework yesterday (past tense)" or, "Please took (past tense) my picture now (present tense)" all sound pretty silly. You have to match up what's happening with when it's happening.

The biggest **Magic Nugget** of all here is that our ears (not our eyes) will usually tell us what is correct. A sentence with the wrong tense or that isn't plural to plural will grate on our nerves. It doesn't "sound" right. Why doesn't it sound right? Because unless you were raised in Nonsense Land, you have been hearing these phrases said correctly thousands and thousands of times by newscasters, teachers, business people, actors (unless they're playing a very odd role), talk show hosts, and (hopefully) parents. Our brain knows what "sounds" right. That's usually all that's needed to find the error, so trust your ears.

There are two exceptions to this technique. The first is any contraction with "have" as the second word in the contraction. Examples are would've, should've, could've, etc. Sometimes the test will ask you to substitute "should of" for "should've". Said aloud and quickly, they sound very much the same. Just think about saying both words in the contraction.

The second exception is the use of a "question" word in the middle of a sentence instead of "that". Question words are who, what, when where, why, and how. An example would be, "There were two people who went to the zoo." The word "who" should be replaced with "that", because the sentence is not a question. Another example would be, "We went to the zoo where we had fun." The word "where" should be replaced with a conjunction, such as "and", because the sentence is not a question. Unfortunately, many people misuse these words to the point that it has become commonplace to hear it, and it might "sound" correct. Just remember, if you see a question word, it has to be a question.

Essay

The Math section is the only section approached with more dread than the essay section. Luckily, it is optional on the ACT and soon will be on the SAT. With that in mind, let's talk briefly about some **Magic Nuggets** for the essay.

The essay need not cause any extra stress. In fact, the essay should be one of the least stressful sections. It is the only section that can be pre-programmed and practically written prior to taking the test. In addition, the time spent grading each essay amounts to about one tenth of the amount of time it takes to write it (if that), so the grading criteria must, by design, be very narrow in scope and shallow in content.

So, what does all of this mean to the essay writer? It means that you should focus on very few things and practice writing them before the test. Each essay question will state an opinion and then ask you to express and support your opinion about their opinion. The key is to state your opinion unequivocally and support it well.

Did I mention that the essay is an opinion about an opinion? Well, then the first **Magic Nugget** is the facts don't matter, so use lots of them to support your opinion. In fact, the graders are not allowed to use accuracy of facts in their grading evaluation.

It matters not what opinion you have, but rather that you support it well. For instance, the opinion stated could be that no good thing has ever come from war. Now whether you agree or disagree is irrelevant. It only matters that you take a side and support it, so choose a side. Now support it with every "fact" that you can imagine.

If you decide that you agree with the above opinion, support it with General W. T. Sherman's quote that, "War is hell, and should never be used as an excuse to kill. In fact, can't we all just get along?" If you decide that you disagree with the opinion, support it with General Sherman's quote that, "War is hell, but hell has forged many good men in the furnace of strife. The world needs more good men, and good men need a place to go have fun when they're not killing each other." That's why General Sherman started the YMCA. Without the War of 1812, the YMCA might never have been created!

Of course, neither of those quotes is accurate. In fact, the second quote is used to support the statement that Sherman created the YMCA (which he didn't) as a result of the War of 1812 (in which he did not fight). The actual quote is, "It is only those who have neither fired a shot nor heard the shrieks and groans of the wounded who cry aloud for blood, more vengeance, more desolation. War is hell."

Now be honest. How many of you checked to see if the third quote was correct? Here's another "be honest." How many of you weren't sure if one or both of the first two quotes were correct before I told you? The point is it doesn't matter. As long as it supports your position, any quote will do, because the facts don't matter.

Here's another **Magic Nugget** that you may have guessed – use a quote from a famous person. A quote from a famous person looks impressive and adds credibility to your position. Also, use one that supports your position, even if you have to make it up. After all, as Abraham Lincoln once said, "Only a foolish man fails to avail himself of all possible advantages, especially with all of the access to the internet these days!" While this may seem to be ridiculous, the essay is NOT being judged on accuracy. It is being judged on having a clear point of view, adequate support of your position, and logical structure. This means that your essay can be a complete work of fiction.

The third **Magic Nugget** is to use your vocabulary words. We'll talk more about vocabulary in the Reading Comprehension chapter, but it is also useful here. Sprinkle adroit, malicious, consternation, arbitrary, or recalcitrant into your essay. If you know what the words mean, it isn't difficult to weave them into your support verbiage, and they will jump off of the page into the eyes of the grader. The grader is scanning and will scan right past "angry old man," but "recalcitrant curmudgeon" rattles their eyes and screams HIGHER SCORE!

The last **Magic Nugget** is to write out your essay before the test. How can you do this? You don't even know what the question will be, right? Wrong. You already know that you will be asked to give your opinion for or against another opinion, so practice doing that. Pick any topic, and write a four-paragraph essay that clearly states your opinion, has two "facts" supporting it, and then clearly wrap up the conclusion restating your position.

Now, why four paragraphs instead of the traditional five? Because you have a limited amount of time. A strong first paragraph stating your position with two supporting paragraphs and a conclusion paragraph are plenty. It is better to have a thorough four-paragraph essay than a sketchy five-paragraph essay.

34

All right, but where do I find "facts" supporting my position? Simple. Make them up. Remember, the facts don't matter. If I want to support the position that drinking more water is good for you, I can cite statistical research studies that show adults that consume above four quarts of water per day live an average of 20 years longer and have I. Q. scores 30% higher than those adults that drink less than four quarts of water per day. I'll bet you didn't know that, did you? Well, neither did I until I made it up. Of course, that same research concludes that these adults tend to be unemployed, because they get fired for spending too much time in the bathroom! I can use it any way I want, because I made it up. All you do is shape it so that it "conclusively" (not a bad word to use in the essay) supports your "clearly stated" position.

Write several practice essays like this. Sometimes, the crazier you write it, the better, because it frees you up to think and write quickly. Use the same famous person (Abraham Lincoln, Harriet Tubman, Andy Warhol, Franklin Roosevelt, Anne Frank, etc.) in each essay saying something different. Write whatever comes into your head and then support it with made up "facts" and quotes. It is much easier than you think, but it will take a little practice to get used to making up "facts" and being "OK" with it.

Magic Nugget Review

1) Don't be afraid to answer that a sentence needs no change. That will be the case approximately 20% - 25% of the time.

2) Even though it may seem that there could be more than one correct answer, there is only one correct answer, and the distinction usually hinges on the words used around the word or phrase in question.

3) "How many tents make sense?" Make sure that plural or singular match between the subject and verb, that the tense (past, present, or future) matches all words, and that the words make sense when used together.

4) When deciding how to match plural or singular subjects with the matching verb, pay attention to the "s". An army marches, and soldiers march.

5) Our ears, not our eyes, will usually tell us the correct answer. If it "sounds" correct, it most often is correct. However, beware of the contraction trap ("should of" rather than "should've") and the trap using the question word when the sentence is not a question.

6)   The facts don't matter in the writing of your essay. It can be a complete work of fiction, and this gives you the freedom to support your thesis with any "facts" that you can imagine.

7)   Use a quote from a famous person in your essay. The quote need not be accurate. It only has to support your thesis.

8)   Use good vocabulary words in your essay. Sprinkling about 8 – 10 of these words in your essay (used properly, of course) will enhance it considerably.

9)   Practice writing out your essay prior to the test. Become comfortable using imagined quotes and facts to support any thesis that you choose.

Magic Nuggets – Reading Comprehension

Most of the help for the Reading Comprehension section will come in the chapter on the **Brain Accelerator**. However, there are a few **Magic Nuggets** for this chapter. Here is the first. The three most important things to study that will really help your reading comprehension is first vocabulary, then second there is vocabulary, and then third is, uh, oh yeah, third is VOCABULARY!

This may seem simple and obvious, but I cannot stress the importance of enhancing your vocabulary enough. Too many students rely on their current vocabulary which borders on pathetic. I don't know if the reason is that less reading is required, text language is too pervasive and very undemanding, or the alien race that created all of the video games being played by humans over the last 20 years implanted a vocabulary eating device into the software. It's probably a combination of all three. In any case, without an expanded vocabulary, tackling the Reading Comprehension section is like trying to row a boat with a teaspoon!

I am constantly told by students when we do practice tests that they did not answer a question or guessed at it, because they did not know what the words meant in the question or the answers. It was as if they had been written in a foreign language. The really sad part is that were it not for the need to study vocabulary words for the SAT or ACT, most students would have no interest in expanding their vocabulary. Most have rarely, if ever, used a dictionary or thesaurus in any form within the last 5 years prior to high school graduation. Let me encourage and challenge you, dear reader, to look up any words that you have seen in this book for which you do not know the meaning. Do it as you read them. That way you can deduce the correct meaning based on its context, and your vocabulary will expand.

The ray of light in this dark cavern of reading horrors is that the problem is easily fixed. Most SAT and ACT study guides have lists of vocabulary words. These lists can also easily be found online. Get a list of about 250 words with their definitions, and make it a priority to learn just five new words each day - just five new words. You'll exhaust your list in about five to six weeks, since a portion of the words will not be new. That's all it takes, but the discipline is doing it each and every day.

Another **Magic Nugget** concerns a particular type of question. It is the EXCEPT question. The EXCEPT question goes something like this, "According to paragraph 3, the author believes all of the following EXCEPT." Skip all EXCEPT questions until all of the other questions have been answered (or at least attempted), because they will take the longest time to answer. All other questions have one correct answer that you must find. The EXCEPT questions have three (ACT) or four (SAT) correct answers that you must find, and you must find them all to eliminate the answer that does not exist. You must do three or four times the amount of work for the same single point earned on the other questions, so if there are any questions left to the end that must be guessed on (ACT) or left unanswered (SAT), let it be the EXCEPT questions.

Magic Nugget Review

1)   Vocabulary, vocabulary, vocabulary! Expand your vocabulary!

2)   Skip the "EXCEPT" until the end. They count the same as all other questions, but they require three to four times as much work.

Magic Nuggets – Math

Math is the section that the majority of students dread the most. This section strikes the most fear into students, because the section is very diverse (basic Arithmetic, Algebra I and II, Coordinate Geometry, Plane Geometry, Data Analysis, and Trigonometry on the ACT), it covers concepts that the students haven't used for years (and if you don't use it, you lose it), and finally, Math is a foundational subject. Each concept builds a foundation for the next concept. Unfortunately, too many students missed a brick or two when building their foundations, and it has hindered (in some cases crippled) them ever since.

Consequently, the Math section has the most **Magic Nuggets**. If you use them, the Math section will lose much of its mystery and dread.

The **Magic Nuggets** I'm going to give you are no substitute for understanding the concepts, but in many cases they will highlight the concepts that are used extensively. That way you can focus on those areas of weakness, if necessary. The other **Magic Nuggets** will help you solve problems much faster by providing short cuts or a simpler, more understandable way to work through the problems.

Some of the **Magic Nuggets** may seem too basic or simple to be important, but I include them, because too many students don't get them. They gloss over the "easy" stuff they learned in grade school, and it comes back to haunt them.

Basic Arithmetic

Know the rules of basic Arithmetic is the first **Magic Nugget**. Know the order of operations and rules of operations. In case you've forgotten, even times anything equals even, odd times odd equals odd, positive times positive and negative times negative both equal positive, positive times negative equals negative, etc. The questions take many forms, but they always start out identifying some variable as an integer. If they instruct you to end up with an even result, it is usually multiplied by some multiple of 2, such as 2, 4, or 6. If they instruct you to end up with a positive result, the integer is usually squared, since negative times negative and positive times positive are always positive.

There is usually a question or two regarding consecutive integers. Consecutive integers are a group of integers listed in order with no gaps. This could be 1, 2, 3 or 2, 4, 6 (even) or 3, 5, 7 (odd). However, the question is generally worded something like this, "The sum of 5 consecutive odd integers is 65. What is the product of the 2 smallest consecutive odd integers?" Well, before you can multiply the two smallest integers to get the product, you must know what all of them are. Where do you start? You can start by adding 1 + 3 + 5 + 7 + 9 and shifting up until you find the right combination (too much wasted time), or you can find the average. 65 divided by 5 equals 13. 13 is your middle integer. The others are 9, 11, 15, and 17. 9 times 11 equals 99, so that is your answer. Next **Magic Nugget**: the average is always the middle number of consecutive integers when there are an odd number of integers. When there are an even number of consecutive integers (rarely used), the average is between the two middle integers.

When multiplying fractions, the rule is multiply the top (numerator) times the top and the bottom (denominator) times the bottom. No problem there, right? Except that this can result in some really big numbers that must then be simplified back down to get the correct answer. Do yourself a big favor. Use the next **Magic Nugget** which is to simplify BEFORE you multiply. For example, consider this common probability without replacement problem:

$$\frac{10}{20} \times \frac{9}{19} \times \frac{8}{18} = \frac{720}{6,840}$$

Or

$$\frac{10}{20} \times \frac{9}{19} \times \frac{8}{18} = \frac{1x1x8}{2x2x9} = \frac{2}{19}$$

In the first example, we simply multiplied the numerators together and the denominators together to get the result, 720 over 6,840. This can be very intimidating to simplify. However, if we simplify 10 over 20 to 1 over 2, 9 over 18 to 1 over 2, 8 over 2 times 2 (4) to 2 over 1, then we end up with the correct answer, 2 over 19. No muss, no fuss!

The next **Magic Nugget** is to know the language of Math. Both the SAT and ACT will use terms in word problems that have a very specific meaning in Math. For instance, a difference is the answer to a subtraction problem. It is not a distinguishing characteristic. A product is the answer to a multiplication problem. It is not something made by a company to sell. In the phrase 20% of a certain number is half the difference of that certain number from 5, "of" means multiply, "certain number" means a variable, "is" means equals, "half" means divide by 2, and "difference" means subtract the variable from 5. The equation would read:

$$20\% \times Y = (5 - Y)/2$$

If you don't know the language, then you can't understand the questions.

Ratios show the relation (in numbers) of one group to another. A ratio of 2:1 between apples and oranges tells you there are 2 times as many apples as oranges. If there are 18 pieces of fruit total, you can use the next **Magic Nugget** to find the amount of each by adding the ratio parts (2 + 1 = 3) and dividing this sum into the total (18/3 = 6) to find the multiplier. Use this multiplier to find either amount (6 x 2 =12 apples and 6 x 1 = 6 oranges).

A cousin of the ratio is the "there are 50 more boys than girls" type of problem. It comes in many varieties, but the question is the same, "How many do I have of each (or one or the other)?" It is easily solved. You simply (**Magic Nugget**) subtract the difference from the total and divide by 2. This gives you the smaller group. Add the difference back, and you have the larger group. Example: In a class of 45 students there are 15 more girls than boys. How many boys are there? $45 - 15 = 30$, $30/2 = 15$ (number of boys), $15 + 15 = 30$ (number of girls).

Averages create a unique problem. Averages seem to be real numbers that give you real information, but they really don't. Averages hide information. For instance, if I have 3 apples, the number 3 is real information. However, if I have a group of people that "average" 3 apples each, do I have 2 people with 6 apples total or 100 people with 300 apples total? The answer, of course, is yes. It could be either one.

Here's another example. In basketball, if a player is fouled while in the act of shooting, that player is awarded foul shots. However, if the player was injured when fouled, the coach may choose any reserve player currently not in the game to shoot the foul shots for the injured player. It is a tie game with 10 seconds left. If the coach looks to his bench and sees player A that is making 100% of his foul shots, and he sees player B that is making 80% of his foul shots, should he choose player A or player B? Who would you choose? The logical choice seems to be player A; however, I neglected to give you all of the information. Player A has only shot one foul shot all year (making it), and player B has shot 200 foul shots (making 160). Now who should he choose?

To combat this problem with averages, use the next **Magic Nugget** which is to always find the "real" numbers. The "real" numbers are the number of things or events (players, tests, homes, etc.) and the total sum of the numbers (scores, shots made, ages, etc.) that you are averaging. To find average, you must divide the total sum by the number of things. To find the number of things, divide the total sum by the average. Lastly, to find the total sum, multiply the number of things by the average. Now use the total sum and number of things. These are your real numbers.

Here's a simple example to show how this works. Joe makes chairs for a living. He wants to average making 5 chairs per day. If he has averaged 4 chairs per day for the first four days, how many chairs must he make on day 5 to meet his goal? The simple and obvious (and wrong) answer is 6, since 5 is the average of 4 and 6. If Joe wants to average 5 chairs per day for 5 days, he must make 25 chairs (5 x 5) total. However, he has only made 16 (4 x 4), so he must make 9 chairs on day 5 in order to have 25 chairs total for the five days.

Here's another "average" problem. A race car travels 1 lap around a 1 mile oval track at an average speed of 30 miles per hour. What speed must the car average on the second lap to average 60 miles per hour for the 2 laps? Most people would answer 90 miles per hour or even 120 miles per hour, but the true answer is that it is impossible. If a car travels 2 laps around a 1 mile track while averaging 60 miles per hour (1 mile per minute), it requires 2 minutes of travel time. Unfortunately, the driver spent 2 minutes going 1 mile at 30 miles per hour. There is no time left to drive the second lap.

Probabilities are pretty straightforward problems. The probability of an event happening is the total number of wanted (or good) outcomes divided by the total number of possible outcomes. For instance, when flipping a coin, the probability of the coin landing with heads up is 1 out of 2 or 50%. It would be the same for tails. Confusion happens when you have multiple tosses or multiple events, so here's the next **Magic Nugget**. If the question says or implies that one event must happen AND another event must happen, then you MULTIPLY the probabilities of the two (or more) events. If the question says or implies that one event must happen OR another event must happen, then you must ADD the probabilities.

Lastly, here's something the study guides rarely cover: logic questions. Logic questions always start with a given statement, and you must pick another statement that is ALWAYS true if the given statement is true. Here's the **Magic Nugget**. The given and answer statements are always in the form of, "If condition A, then result B. If NOT result B, then NOT condition A." The question will give one of these sentences, and you must find the other. I added the emphasis to "not" (they won't), because it is a key to the order of the condition and result. The statement with "not" has the order of the condition and result reversed from the original. You MUST have this reversal to be correct.

51

Algebra

Probably the biggest obstacle that most students have in Algebra is factoring quadratic equations. Quadratic equations come in the basic form of $ax^2 + bx + c$, where a, b, and c are integers. Factoring quadratics is not difficult if you follow a few basic steps, but it is ABSOLUTELY NECESSARY to know how to do it. Many of the questions hinge on this skill.

This **Magic Nugget** will outline the steps involved in factoring, and then we will look at some of the applications.

Step 1. Factor out any number or variable common to all of the terms. For example: $2x^2 + 6x + 4$ becomes $2(x^2 + 3x + 2)$.

Step 2. Draw 2 sets of parentheses under the equation.

Step 3. Determine the signs in the parentheses, and put them inside. How do you determine the signs? If the last sign in the quadratic is positive, then both signs will be the same, so look at the middle sign in the quadratic and duplicate it in the parentheses. If, however, the last sign is negative, then there will be one of each sign in the parentheses. For example: the expression $x^2 + 6x + 8$ has a positive last sign and positive middle sign, so both signs are positive. The expression $x^2 - 6x + 8$ has a positive last sign and negative middle sign, so both signs are negative. Lastly, the expression $x^2 + 7x - 8$ has a negative last sign, so there will be one of each sign.

Step 4. Factor the corners. The corners are the integers "a" and "c" in our basic quadratic equation $ax^2 + bx + c$. Usually "a" will be a 1, so no factoring is required. Factor "c" starting with 1 and its pair, then increase the factors until they meet in the middle. For example: the factors of 12 are 1 & 12, 2 & 6, and 3 & 4. We don't need to go past 3 & 4, because 4 & 3 is the same.

Step 5. Find the correct pair of factors and put them in the parentheses. If both signs in the parentheses are the same, then look for a pair of factors whose SUM is "b" or the middle number. If the signs are different, then look for a pair of factors whose DIFFERENCE is "b". For example, in $x^2 + 6x + 8$, the factors of 8 are 1 & 8 and 2 & 4. $2 + 4 = 6$, so 2 & 4 are used. In $x^2 + 4x - 12$, where the factors of 12 are 1 & 12, 2 & 6, and

3 & 4, **6 – 2 = 4**, so 6 & 2 are used. When "b" is positive, put the largest factor behind the plus sign in the parentheses. When "b" is negative, put the largest factor behind the minus sign. See Table II for some applications of these steps.

Table II

Quadratic Factoring Applications

Examples	$x^2 - 6x + 8$	$2x^2 - 12x - 32$
Step 1	$x^2 - 6x + 8$	$2(x^2 - 6x - 16)$
Step 2	( )( )	( ) ( )
Step 3	(-)(-)	(+) (-)
Step 4	1 & 8	1 & 16
	2 & 4	2 & 8
		4 & 4
Step 5	$(x - 4)(x - 2)$	$2(x + 2)(x - 8)$

The "difference of squares" is a very commonly used quadratic. It comes in the form of $a^2 - b^2$, where each term is a perfect square and they are subtracted (hence the "difference").

Magic Nugget: $a^2 - b^2$ is ALWAYS factored $(a + b) (a - b)$. You may see it in both forms: factored and unfactored. If you can recognize it quickly, you will save time solving the problem.

Simultaneous equations always involve 2 unknowns (variables) and 2 equations. They are solved using substitution or elimination. You will need to know both, but the **Magic Nugget** here is recognizing a simultaneous equation. Whenever there are 2 unknowns interrelated to each other (i.e., the value of one affects the value of the other), then this is a simultaneous equation problem, and you must not only identify the two unknowns, but you must also identify the two equations. Sometimes the latter task is more difficult. Consider this word problem. George goes to the Farmer's Market and buys 10 pieces of fruit to make a fruit salad. If apples are 50 cents each and pears are 1 dollar each, how many apples did George buy if he spent $6.50?

The two unknowns are obviously the amounts of apples (A) and pears (P). The obvious first equation is .50A + 1.00P = 6.50, but what is the second equation? The second equation is A + P = 10 (the number of pieces of fruit purchased). <u>If there are two unknowns, then there MUST be two equations.</u>

Geometry

Geometry is an emotional subject for most people – love it or hate it. It is also quite different from Arithmetic and Algebra, because it relies much less on numbers. Geometry is about relationships. It is puzzle-solving. Consequently, the **Magic Nuggets** are going to be about solving the puzzle faster by taking a shortcut. It is something like knowing where the passages to different levels are located in a video game.

<u>Parallel lines</u> show up early and often on both the SAT and ACT. The **Magic Nugget** here is that <u>if they state that there are parallel lines, then you can be 100% sure that the answer hinges on that fact.</u>

<u>Parallel lines with a transversal</u> (a line crossing them) create two types of angles: congruent (equal measure) and

supplementary (angles whose measures add up to 180°).
Supplementary angles come into play about 10% - 20% of the
time with regards to parallel lines. Congruent angles make up
the vast majority with one particular type being used almost
every time.

There are four types of congruent angles (see Figure 1 for
the corresponding letters): Vertical a/d, Corresponding a/e,
Alternate Interior c/f, and Alternate Exterior a/h. Of these four
types of congruent angles, the alternate interior angles are used

Figure 1

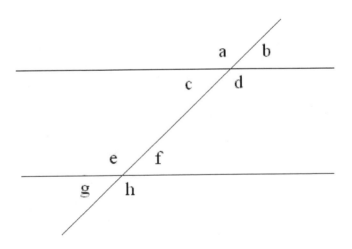

the most often. Why? Because (**Magic Nugget**) they are the
only type contained BETWEEN the parallel lines. When a

figure is used, such as a parallelogram, there are no angles outside the figure. All of the angles are WITHIN the figure, so look immediately for the alternate interior angles.

There are all kinds of triangles, but the type you see almost all of the time are right triangles. Because of this, you need to know the Pythagorean Theorem backwards and forwards. The equation $a^2 + b^2 = c^2$ will be used often. However, you can shortcut this if you know and recognize the special right triangles. These triangles are special, because we can figure out the side measurements without using the Pythagorean Theorem.

There are two types of special right triangles. The first type is a right triangle where the angle measurements are known. There are two of these: an isosceles right triangle (also known as a 45/45 right triangle), and the second is a 30/60/90 right triangle. On both of these triangles, we know the angle measurements and the ratios of the sides.

The isosceles right triangle, or 45/45, has 2 sides the same length: hence, the isosceles designation. We also know that the sides of a triangle are proportionate in length to the angles opposite to them, so sides with the same length have angles opposite to them with the same measurement. In this case, we know they are 45°, because the third angle is 90°, and the sum of the interior angles of any triangle is 180°. As you can see in Figure 2, the sides forming the right angle are the same (variable x), and the hypotenuse is $x\sqrt{2}$. So, if the side

Figure 2

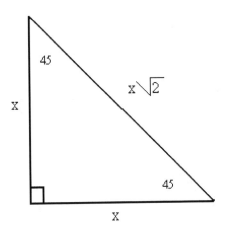

measures 5, the hypotenuse will measure $5\sqrt{2}$. Conversely, if you know that the hypotenuse measures $6\sqrt{2}$, then the two sides measure 6.

That's all well and good. In fact, the SAT will give you those ratios at the beginning of each Math test. But what do you do if you know the hypotenuse measures 8? That's not in the format of x $\sqrt{2}$. No problem. Here's a **Magic Nugget** for that. When you have an integer as the measure of the hypotenuse, divide it by 2 and multiply by $\sqrt{2}$ to get the measure of the sides. If the hypotenuse is 8, then the sides are $4\sqrt{2}$.

There are several indicators that should alert you that a 45/45 triangle is being used. Obviously a right angle and 45° angle in the triangle is one alert. Another is the right isosceles triangle designation that may be given to it in the question. The least obvious, but often used, indicator that a 45/45 triangle is in play (**Magic Nugget**) is the identification of the figure used as a square. A diagonal drawn from corner to corner in a square creates two 45/45 triangles, and the square is often used as a set-up to bring in the 45/45 triangle. The question may give the length of the diagonal of the square and ask for the area of the square or some other measurement that will require you to use the side ratios of the 45/45 triangle in order to calculate the answer. In any case, when you see square in the question, immediately think 45/45 triangle.

The 30/60/90 triangle is the other right triangle with known side ratios as shown in Figure 3. These ratios are also included at the beginning of the SAT Math tests. Using these

Figure 3

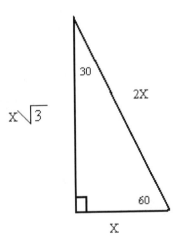

ratios, if the hypotenuse is 12, the short side (opposite the 30^0 angle) is 6, and the long side (opposite the 60^0 angle) is $6\sqrt{3}$. Again, all well and good if the measurements conform to the model shown. However, if the long side is an integer (**Magic**

Nugget), simply divide it by 3 and multiply by $\sqrt{3}$ to obtain the length of the short side. Then multiply by 2 to get the length of the hypotenuse. For example, if the long side is 9, the short side is $3\sqrt{3}$, and the hypotenuse is $6\sqrt{3}$.

Just like the 45/45 triangle, the 30/60/90 has indicators, as well. Obviously a right triangle with either a 30° or 60° angle is a 30/60/90 triangle. A less obvious indicator (**Magic Nugget**) is the use of an equilateral triangle. An equilateral triangle with an altitude (a perpendicular bisecting line segment from any vertex of the triangle to the opposite side) creates two 30/60/90 triangles. When a question says that a triangle is equilateral, you start thinking 30/60/90 triangle.

The second type of special right triangle is known as a Pythagorean Triple. A Pythagorean Triple is a right triangle with integer measurements for all three sides. The easiest to remember and most often used is the 3/4/5 triple. This triple comes in many flavors, since all of the multiples of the 3/4/5 are valid as well. For example, any triangle with sides of 6/8/10, 12/16/20, 30/40/50, etc. is a 3/4/5. Another commonly seen triple is the 5/12/13 and its multiples.

The significance of the triple is that you don't need to use the Pythagorean Theorem to find the third side when you know the first two sides. This CONSIDERABLY reduces the amount of time needed to solve a problem that uses one of these triples.

Again, the most commonly used and easiest to recognize is the 3/4/5. It will be used many times on the test, and (**Magic Nugget**) the easiest way to recognize it is by looking at the hypotenuse. <u>If the hypotenuse is a multiple of 5, then divide it by 5 to find the multiplier. Then divide the other known side by the multiplier. If the result is a 3 or 4, then the triangle is a 3/4/5</u>. If the hypotenuse is unknown, but the other two sides are multiples of 3 and 4 with the same multiplier, then the hypotenuse is 5 times the multiplier.

The SAT and ACT both use circles (and semi-circles) to create some interesting problems. Something to remember is that a line tangent to a circle is perpendicular to the radius of the circle at the point of tangency. This phenomenon creates right triangles which really makes these Pythagorean Theorem or Pythagorean Triple type problems.

The more difficult and obscure problems using circles involve a circle inscribed in a square (Figure 4) or a square inscribed in a circle (Figure 5). In Figure 4, (**Magic Nugget**) the dotted line is the diameter of the circle. It is also the same length as the SIDE of the square. In Figure 5, (**Magic Nugget**) the dotted line is also the diameter of the circle, but this time it is the DIAGONAL (remember the 45/45 triangle) of the square. These measurements are used to either find dimensions of the square or dimensions of the circle. Remember that the diameter of the circle is twice the length of the radius, and it is the radius that is used in circle equations for area and circumference.

Figure 4   **Figure 5**

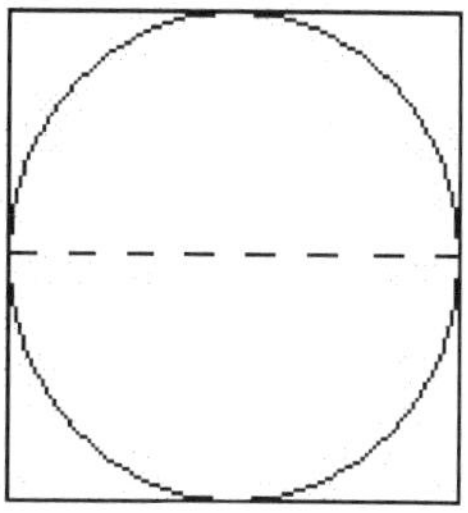

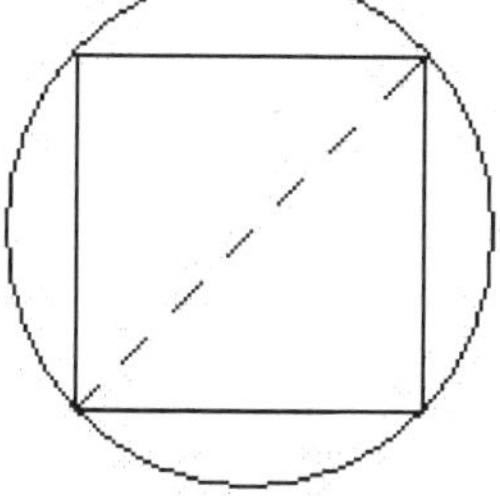

When it comes to Coordinate Geometry, it is helpful to remember the midpoint formula (Figure 6), the distance formula (Figure 7), and the slope formula (Figure 8), but it is

essential to know the slope intercept form of a linear function,

which is $y = mx + b$. The variable "m" is the slope, and the

variable "b" is the y intercept. This equation is used to identify

graphs, identify parallel functions (the slope is equal), and

identify perpendicular functions (the original slope = m, and the

perpendicular slope equals the negative reciprocal or -1/m).

Figure 6   Midpoint (x , y) (X1 + X2)/2 , (Y1+Y2)/2

Figure 7   Distance $=\sqrt{(X2-X1)^2 + (Y2-Y1)^2}$

Figure 8   Slope = rise/run   Slope = (Y2 − Y1)/(X2 - X1)

Here's one further note about Coordinate Geometry. If

given two points on a graph (or two ordered pairs of

coordinates), many times it is quicker and easier to find the

distance between those points by making that line segment the

hypotenuse of a right triangle (**Magic Nugget**) rather than using

the distance formula. Point coordinates readily give you the length of the two legs, and you can use the Pythagorean Theorem, or many times you find that the triangle created is a 3/4/5 triple. For instance, if you need to find the distance between points (2,3) and (5,7), you can calculate that the horizontal leg is length 3 (5 − 2), and the vertical leg is length 4 (7 − 3). This means the length of the hypotenuse must be 5, and that is the distance between points (2,3) and (5,7).

Trigonometry

The ACT test contains four questions on Trigonometry. These questions may seem complex, but they generally are not as long as you know SOH CAH TOA (**Magic Nugget**). No, that's not some famous Indian chief. That is an acronym for the three primary Trigonometry ratios. Sine equals the Opposite side measurement over the Hypotenuse measurement, Cosine equals the Adjacent side measurement over the Hypotenuse measurement, and Tangent equals the Opposite side measurement over the Adjacent side measurement. If you understand these ratios, then at least three out of the four questions will be easy.

Here's a few minor **Magic Nuggets**. Tangent also equals Sine over Cosine. Also, if you have to isolate an unknown variable that is in the denominator, merely switch it with the value on the other side of the equation. For instance, if you must solve for the hypotenuse, as in Figure 9, the equation would originate like this: $\sin \Theta = 14/x$. Switch $\sin \Theta$ with x to look like this: $x = 14/\sin\Theta$.

Figure 9

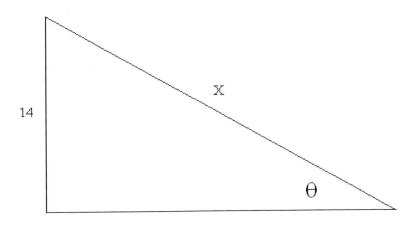

This last **Magic Nugget** will eliminate one calculation. That may not seem like much, but each calculation is an opportunity to make an error. If you only make an error on 5% of your calculations, and you are able to eliminate only one calculation (most of the **Magic Nuggets** save more than one calculation) from only two thirds of the Math questions, you will eliminate two wrong answers. That alone will add 20 points to your SAT score and 1 point to your ACT score!

Magic Nugget Review

1) Know the rules of basic Arithmetic. They will be used often, and most students have forgotten many of them.

2) The "average" of a list of consecutive integers is always the middle integer.

3) When multiplying fractions, always simplify before you multiply.

4) Know the language of Math. Word problems become much easier if you know specifically what the question is requesting or instructing you to do.

5) When solving ratio problems, add the ratio parts of the given groups, divide the total of the groups by this sum, and use this result as a multiplier to find the amounts in each group.

6) When solving a "more than" problem involving two groups, subtract the "more than" amount from the total and divide the result by 2. This will give the lesser amount. Add the "more than" amount to the lesser amount to find the greater amount.

7) When solving problems involving averages, always use the "real" numbers: total and number of things. Use these numbers to calculate your answer rather than using the averages.

8) On a probability question with multiple events, multiply the probabilities if it says "and", and add the probabilities if it says "or".

9) On logic questions, the two statements that are linked will be in the form, "If condition A, then result B. If not result B, then not condition A."

10) It is absolutely necessary to know how to factor quadratic expressions. Table II illustrates the steps.

11) The "difference of squares" always comes in the form $a^2 - b^2$, and it is always factored $(a + b)(a - b)$. Know it forwards and backwards, because it is used often in many ways.

12) Whenever there are two interrelated unknowns in a problem, it must be solved using elimination or substitution with two equations.

13) If a question states that parallel lines are being used, then you can be 100% sure that the answer hinges on that fact.

14) The alternate interior angle is the most important type of angle when dealing with figures that have parallel lines, because it is the only type that exists entirely between the parallel lines.

15) When an integer is the measure of the hypotenuse of a 45/45 right triangle, divide the integer by 2 and multiply by $\sqrt{2}$ to find the measure of the sides.

16) When a question identifies a figure to be used in the problem as a square, immediately look for the application of the 45/45 right triangle ratios.

17) When an integer is the measure of the long leg (opposite the 60 degree angle) in a 30/60/90 right triangle, divide that integer by 3 and multiply by $\sqrt{3}$ to get the short leg. Double that value to get the hypotenuse.

18) When a question identifies a figure to be used in the problem as an equilateral triangle, immediately look for the application of the 30/60/90 right triangle ratios.

19) The 3/4/5 Pythagorean triple is used often on the test, and the easiest way to identify its possible existence is that the measure of the hypotenuse is a multiple of 5.

20) When a circle is inscribed in a square, the diameter of the circle is equal to the measure of the side of the square.

21) When a square is inscribed in a circle, the measure of the diagonal of the square is equal to the diameter of the circle.

22) When calculating the distance between two points in the x y plane, it is usually faster and more accurate to form a right triangle with the hypotenuse forming the line between the two points. Then use the Pythagorean Theorem or Pythagorean triple properties to calculate the distance.

23) Know the definition and uses of SOH CAH TOA.

24) Tangent also equals sine divided by cosine.

25) When the variable that needs to be isolated is in the denominator of a fraction, switch it with the value on the other side of the equal sign.

Magic Nuggets - Science Reasoning

The ACT test also includes a separate test on <u>Science Reasoning</u>. If you are not especially good at Science, there's no need to worry. While the questions asked use scientific subjects as the backdrop, you really need very little, if any, science training.

What you do need is an understanding of charts, graphs, and tables. In other words, it's Coordinate Geometry, again! I know some of you are cheering, and some of you are wailing and gnashing your teeth. It's actually much easier than the Math section. It's all about comparisons and "which makes more sense" type of questions. Here's the **Magic Nugget**. <u>Don't over complicate the question in your head</u>. Keep it simple. Compare one value to another. Which one is higher, longer, faster, shorter, etc.? Don't worry about what chemicals or viruses are mentioned. It's just about the comparisons.

Magic Nugget Review

1)   Don't over complicate the Science Reasoning problems. Keep them simple. It's just about comparisons.

Put the Pedal to the Metal!

The Brain Accelerator

Well, I've served you the appetizer, soup, and salad, so here comes the main course. Get ready for a feast!

The techniques I'm about to describe will allow your brain to accelerate and solve MORE problems and do it FASTER than before. How do we do that? By removing the restrictor plate on your brain!

A restrictor plate is a device used in auto racing, primarily NASCAR, to keep a car from going faster by restricting the amount of air that can flow into the engine. The engine uses air to mix with fuel and adds a spark to power the car. The car carries the fuel it needs in the fuel tank, but it must have more air to create more power to go faster.

Well, your brain is like a high-powered race car. It has a store of fuel called memories, and it uses the fresh air of information to mix with the stored memories and a small electrical spark to create the power of ideas and solutions.

However, your brain has a restrictor plate when it comes to the SAT and ACT, and it is called, "How I Take Tests."

The techniques I'm going to give you I formulated over years of helping students prepare for tests. When I found a technique that worked, I kept it. When it didn't, I discarded it. Over the years, the techniques became more and more effective. I was helping students make monumental leaps in their scores, and I intuitively knew that there must be a scientific basis for the results. So, I started to research the brain, and I found studies done by neuroscientists describing the processes of the brain (specifically regarding memory and learning) that explained why my techniques were so successful.

Before I describe the techniques, I need to share what I found out about the brain – your brain – and how it works. This will help you "buy-in" to the techniques. I promise to make it interesting and easy to understand.

Your brain has two parts that process information: the conscious mind and the subconscious mind. Your conscious mind works like a computer. A computer takes a piece of information, either from data storage or from an outside source, and processes it. Computers do this very fast, so it seems as though it is doing many things simultaneously, but the central processing unit (CPU) of a computer can only process one piece of information at a time. It then passes that piece of information to the working (or short-term) memory to be used again soon or sends it to long-term memory, like a disc drive, for use at some later date.

Your conscious mind works practically the same way. It takes a piece of information from memory or an outside source (sight, hearing, taste, touch, and smell) and processes it one piece at a time before sending it to short-term working memory or deeper into long-term memory. When you "focus" on something, you are using your conscious mind. Again, this happens very fast.

However, unlike a computer, your brain also has a subconscious mind working in the background, and it can work on many tasks at once. Your subconscious mind is processing everything that your conscious mind is not currently processing. These two parts of your mind work together, and they work separately.

To demonstrate this to yourself, look around the room that you are occupying. Find something interesting on which to focus. It might be a lamp, a painting, or anything else that catches your eye. Now focus only on that object. Notice its color, shape, size etc. Now close your eyes, think back, and remember all the things you saw, heard, felt, smelled, or tasted that had NOTHING to do with the object you picked as your focus. See? Your subconscious mind was busy gathering all that information on which your conscious mind was not "focused," because your subconscious mind can process many things at once, while your conscious mind cannot.

Here's another way that your subconscious mind works that is different from your conscious mind. When you choose to focus on something with your conscious mind, whatever you were focusing on previously is now not being processed. Remember, you can only focus on one thing at a time, so your conscious mind has to quit "working" on whatever it just dismissed. However, your subconscious mind continues to grind away on it. If it was a question or problem of some sort, your subconscious mind will work on the problem until it either finds the answer or discovers that it does not have the answer.

It might take a few minutes, an hour, or days, but your subconscious mind will exhaust all resources before it lets go.

Don't believe me? How many times have you seen a movie, television program, commercial, etc. and said to yourself, "Who is that actor? I know that voice!" or "I know that face!" No matter how hard you focus on that person, you can't remember their name. It's "on the tip of your tongue," but it won't come out, so you release focusing on the thought. Then five minutes, 30 minutes, a couple hours, or even a couple of days later, the answer pops into your head! You weren't thinking of that actor at all, but as soon as your subconscious mind had solved the mystery, it sent the information back to your conscious mind on a silver platter!

It is these inherent characteristics of your subconscious mind that allow it to gather lots of information and process it autonomously while you are focusing on something else entirely that make your subconscious mind the **REAL** problem solver. A study done in 2007 at Wake Forest University Baptist Medical Center found that "making the right choice" does not necessarily come from conscious deliberation. A better choice was usually rendered from subconscious thinking. In fact, it was found that the more complex the problem, the better the subconscious mind handled it compared to the conscious mind.

Dr. W. R. Klemm, Phd., is a Senior Professor of Neuroscience at Texas A & M University. He has written 18 books and numerous other scholarly works on memory and learning. One excellent book of his on memory and learning is titled, "*Memory Power 101: A Comprehensive Guide to Better Learning for Students, Businesspeople, and Seniors.*" In it he states, "… simple decisions are best made by careful conscious thought. But for complicated decisions, the best choices may result from 'deliberation without paying attention,' that is letting the thinking be done by the subconscious mind."

So what does all of this have to do with scoring significantly higher on the SAT and ACT tests? **EVERYTHING!** Remember your brain's restrictor plate called, "How I Take Tests"? Well, that restrictor plate almost entirely blocks the use of your subconscious mind, and like the restrictor plate on a race car, it severely limits how well and how fast your brain can answer the questions on the test.

So how does this restrictor plate work, and, more importantly, how do you get rid of it? Again, the restrictor plate on a race car restricts airflow, and your brain's restrictor plate restricts information. "How I Take Tests" has been taught to you over and over throughout the years, and it goes something like this, "Focus on one problem at a time. Do the problems in order, unless you get stuck on a problem and can't solve it. After unsuccessfully trying to solve it, skip it and continue solving the other problems in order. If you have extra time, you can come back to the problem(s) you skipped and give it one last ditch effort. That is, of course, if you have time."

That method of taking a sophisticated and complex test is completely and utterly **WRONG**! It does not allow your subconscious mind to work on the problems that it does best – the complex problems. Instead it forces your conscious mind to work on problems for which it was not designed.

The two major sections where this phenomenon is most prevalent are the Reading Comprehension section and the Math section. There are somewhat different techniques for bringing your subconscious mind into full utilization in these sections, but both sets of techniques optimize the use of your subconscious mind. Once you have mastered the techniques (they do take a little practice to do well), your scores can increase dramatically by 20%, 30%, 50%, or more!

Reading Comprehension

On the Reading Comprehension test, you are told to read the passages and answer questions based on those passages. As instructed, you read as fast as you can, and then you try to answer the questions, but you can't really recall much of the passage, at least not enough to answer the questions without doubt, because you read really fast. So you go back and reread the parts of the passage that you think will give you the answers.

Before you know it, your time has expired, and you haven't even LOOKED at the last 10 questions! Sound familiar? What happened? It's simple. You spent almost all of your time reading, and **YOU ONLY FOCUSED ON ONE PROBLEM AT A TIME**.

What do you do? **STOP READING THE PASSAGES**! Wait . . . WHAT? That's right. You need to stop reading the passages and doing things all in sequential order. That only uses your conscious mind, and frankly it overloads it to the point that you even lose what little focus you had. Instead, you need to remove the restrictor plate by changing, "How I Take Tests." You need to bring your subconscious mind into play with all of its added capacity, autonomous work capability, and peripheral information gathering abilities.

Here's how. When the test begins, rather than read the first passage, you read all of the questions. While you are quickly (emphasis on quickly) reading the questions, you underline the key words, phrases, and/or line references. Be frugal with your underlining. If a question has 12 words, don't underline 7 of them. You should underline a maximum of four words (preferably two or three) or a maximum of two phrases (including line references) of two or three words each. Words or phrases that are capitalized or in quotations will make good choices, because they tend to be important and will be easy to find later. Any question that is an EXCEPT question is skipped altogether (as I stated earlier). When you come back to the EXCEPT question, underline the key words or phrases in the ANSWERS, not the question. You do this, because there are multiple true statements that must ALL be found to isolate the false statement.

Once you have your key words or phrases underlined, pick a question and reread the key words and/or phrases. Then take the index finger (pointing finger) of the hand opposite of your writing hand, and place it at the top of the passage and in the middle of the lines (side to side). Now focus on your finger, and slide it down vertically from top to bottom. While you are focusing on your finger, be aware of all of the words that become visible to you as your finger slides down the page. It should take you no longer than four to five seconds to slide it from top to bottom. If there is another column, do the same thing starting at the top in the middle and slide your finger down. I refer to this as scanning.

As your finger slides down the page, you will become aware of all the significant words around the outline of your finger. You are scanning for your key words or phrases. Words like "the", "and", "from", etc. will not catch your eye, but words like "engagement", "suffering", "integration", and "constellation" will jump off of the page at you.

When you find your key word(s) or phrase(s), go back to the question (keep your index finger on the spot), and quickly read the answers. Now go back to where your finger is located, and quickly look for one of the answers that you just read. Almost every time, the answer will be there in the passage virtually word for word. It is amazing how often the answer matches up so well with the passage.

Be aware, however, that sometimes one of the answers may contain words from the passage, but it will not say the same thing as the passage. This usually takes the form of the answer being more specific or containing more information than the passage. This answer is a trap! Here's an example. One of the answers to the question might state, "Gloria's love for dancing and singing lead her to try out for musical plays," while the text might say, "Gloria loved to dance and sing." While it is possible that Gloria did try out for musical plays, the passage does not SAY that she did, so it is an incorrect answer.

Sometimes, especially if the key word(s) or phrase(s) you have underlined are used often in the passage, the first location you find may not contain the answer. No problem. Start scanning again until you find your key word(s) or phrase(s), again, and quickly repeat the process.

When you first begin to learn how to scan, you may go through the entire passage without finding your key word or phrase. Don't panic. It is there. Simply start scanning again, and fight the urge to start reading, because that will only slow you down and lock out your subconscious mind. If you scan again the same as before, a wonderful phenomenon occurs. The words you saw around your finger and recognized the first time blend into the background, because your subconscious mind has processed them and discarded them. Instead, you will recognize and process words further away from your finger effectively doubling or tripling the amount of words that you process. This takes a little practice, but it will come quickly if you devote some time to it.

To show you how powerful your subconscious mind can be when exercised this way, let me share a quick story about one of my former students. This student had a learning disability such that things he read did not easily get absorbed by his mind. He might have to read a page several times just to understand the general message of it. I taught him this method of scanning and encouraged him to practice with books, magazines, newspapers, etc.

One day he showed up for his lesson and said an amazing thing had happened. He worked part-time at a large retail store with literally thousands and thousands of items in inventory. A customer came in requesting a very specific item. His manager handed him a large packet of pages with the entire inventory listed by part number and with a very brief description. She asked him to find the item the customer wanted on the inventory sheets, if he could, and somehow help the customer. He said without thinking about it he started using his finger to scan the pages, and within seconds he found the correct item about 4 pages back. His manager was shocked that he had found it so quickly, and he was amazed at himself when he realized what he had done! The subconscious mind is VERY powerful when allowed to operate unhindered.

For now, there is one small exception on the SAT. After the vocabulary questions, there is a short Reading Comprehension section with two passages of about 6 to 10 lines each. The questions are almost always "compare and contrast" type questions. First, quickly read the questions in order for you to know what to consider, and then quickly read the passages once to get their flavor and tone. It won't take very long, and the passages are short enough that you should remember all you need to know. Remember, you have prepped your mind by quickly reading the questions first. Go with your first impression. Your subconscious mind does not lie to you, but your conscious mind may try to talk you out of it, because it is incapable of processing ALL of the information at once. What you think is a "gut feeling" is really your subconscious mind telling you, "I have weighed all of the information you have given me, and this is the best answer."

Math

The Math section, especially on the SAT, contains probably the most complex questions on the entire test. I have always explained to my students that the most complex Math question is always solved with a series of very simple steps. The key, of course, is knowing which steps to take, and both tests (but especially the SAT) do a pretty good job of disguising and complicating the questions. All the more reason that your subconscious mind MUST be allowed to step in unfettered by "How I Take Tests," because the more complex the problem, the better suited your subconscious mind is to handle it than your conscious mind.

So how do you unleash the awesome power of your subconscious mind on all of those nasty Math questions? You use what I call the **1, 2, 3 Method**. It is simple and elegant in design, but it is extremely effective.

When you are allowed to begin the test, as quickly as possible you read each and every question, but you don't read the answers. In your mind, you classify each question as a **class 1, 2, or 3**. You do this as quickly as possible, and it

93

should take less than one quarter of your allotted time. Therefore, on the ACT, which allots 60 minutes to the Math section, this should be completed in 15 minutes or less.

By definition, a **class 1** question is easily solved by you. It should take you less than 5 seconds to answer – 10 seconds if you have to make a calculation. These questions are very straight forward and perfect for your conscious mind to solve, so you immediately answer all **class 1** questions. Get them out of the way and move on. Don't clutter your mind with **class 1** questions. The **class 1** questions tend to be early in the test, because the questions basically progress on the test from easiest to hardest. However, a later question could be a **class 1** question for you. It just depends on you.

A **class 2** question is one that you know how to solve, but it will take longer than 5 - 10 seconds or more than one calculation to solve. These are the questions that require the most discipline. The urge is usually very strong in you to start solving the problem rather than skipping, but it must be skipped! Time is of the essence, so you must move quickly. **Class 2** questions are scattered throughout the test.

94

A **class 3** question is one that causes your eyes to roll back into your head and your mouth to drop open and exclaim to yourself, "Oh my goodness! I haven't got the foggiest notion what I just read!" These are easy to skip while you try to stop hyperventilating.

Let me just interject something VERY IMPORTANT right here. At no time are you allowed to "jump out of the boat!" What do I mean by "jump out of the boat?" I mean that mentally you CANNOT give up on any question – even the **class 3** questions. You must remain locked in and committed to solving every problem no matter how hard it seems. I will explain why this is so important later.

All right, you've just read the last question, and since the tougher questions tend to be at the end, the first thing you should do is close your mouth. Otherwise, small bugs tend to fly in it. Now consider, "What have you accomplished?" You have accomplished a ton! You just don't know it, yet. You have answered all of the **class 1** questions. It's probably around 10% - 15% of the total number of questions, but don't be discouraged if it is less than 10%. In fact, don't be discouraged if there are ZERO **class 1** questions answered, because you have also completed two additional, more important tasks.

The second task that you have completed is you have taken the mystery out of the test. When you answer questions sequentially, many times panic starts to set in near the end of the test. The time is winding down, you know that there are harder questions ahead, and you have no idea what they will ask you to do! No worries, mate! You've already finished reading all of the questions, so you KNOW what they will ask you. The mystery and associated fear of the unknown are gone.

The third and most important task that you have just completed is you have just loaded ALL of the **class 2** and **class 3** questions into your subconscious mind. Your subconscious mind is now starting to organize the methods needed to solve the mystery of each question. If the information is in your brain, then your subconscious mind will locate it and send it to your conscious mind at the appropriate time and in an orderly fashion.

It is this third task that REALLY tears the restrictor plate off your brain and allows it to operate at maximum speed and efficiency. When you go back to solve the **class 2** questions that you have skipped, your calculations and reasoning will be more organized and faster. You will KNOW how to solve the problem, rather than just THINK you know. Now, this still assumes that you have prepared properly. The race car can't run with an empty fuel tank no matter how much air it gets, and your subconscious mind can't find information in your brain that isn't there.

In addition, remember the **class 3** questions that stopped your breathing and made your eyes roll back into your head? Miraculously, some of them have become **class 2** or even **class 1** questions when you come back to them. You say to yourself, "That's what they were talking about!" That is why you can't jump out of the boat. If you stay committed to solving each and every one of the questions, then your subconscious mind will keep searching for the needed information. If, however, you mentally jump out of the boat, your subconscious mind takes that as an instruction to halt the search before it ever begins! You have clamped that restrictor plate back on your brain, and those **class 3** questions will remain **class 3** forever.

Now, the first pass through, all the question classifications must be accomplished as fast as possible. Again, you want to take no more, and preferably less, than one quarter of your time. Don't worry about making a mistake in your classifications by going too fast. The worst mistake that you can make is you classify a question as **class 2** or **class 3** when it really is a **class 1**. When you come back through, it will still be a **class 1** question, and you will answer it.

The second pass through the test is when you take a little extra time to make sure of your calculations. Also, when you have a "solution," look back at the question, and be sure your "solution" answers the question properly. The SAT and ACT will include "common mistake" answers in their listed choices. That's why you don't read the answers when you read the question. You don't want to bias your subconscious mind before it starts searching for the information.

When you are working on questions during the second pass, draw pictures as much as possible to illustrate the question. Our minds think in pictures, not words. For instance, if I ask you to close your eyes and think of a football, you see in your mind a brown ball that is pointy at both ends (unless

you're European, in which case you will see a soccer ball!).
What you will not see are the letters F – O – O – T – B – A – L
- L.

Drawing pictures organizes your thoughts and crystallizes the problem in your mind. Dr. Klemm explains it this way, "Why are pictures so effective? The explanation lies in the fact that the sensory systems and brain devote far more nerve cells to vision than to any other sense." The estimates of the number of optic nerve fibers going from the eyes to the brain range from 730,000 to 1,700,000. The estimates of the number of auditory nerve fibers going from the ears to the brain range from 28,000 to 30,000.

That means that there are as much as 57 TIMES MORE optic nerve fibers as auditory. Conclusion? DRAW MORE PICTURES!

Also, during the second pass, you will encounter those **class 3** questions. After reading them, if they are still **class 3**, skip them again, but don't give up on them. Your subconscious mind may still find the clues it needs to lead you to the answer if you don't jump out the boat. You simply tell yourself, "I'm not done working on this one," and you move on.

All right. You've gone through the test several times, and the **class 3** questions are still **class 3**. Don't sweat it. Unless you were unprepared, and half of the questions are **class 3**, you should be in pretty good shape. Look at the **class 3** questions, and try to eliminate any obviously wrong answers. Then you guess. On the ACT, you will not leave any question unanswered, because there is no penalty for a wrong answer. On the SAT, only guess if you can intelligently narrow the answers down to two or three possible choices. Otherwise, leave it unanswered.

The SAT penalizes you one quarter of a point for each wrong multiple choice answer (no penalty for a wrong grid-in answer, so put something). However, they also round up each half point to the next full point, so you essentially get two free guesses. For example, if you had 40 correct answers and 2 incorrect answers, your raw score would be 39.5, but they would round it back up to 40.

Whatever you do, DO NOT go back and change any answers. Remember, your subconscious and conscious minds have given you their best efforts. Don't second guess yourself. The only time you would ever consider changing an answer is if you happen to see a mistake in a calculation that would lead you to a wrong solution. Otherwise, you are finished with the test.

An Ounce of Prevention is Worth a Pound of Cure

This may seem like closing the barn door after the cows got out to talk about pre-test preparation at the end of the book, but the book is really about taking the test. However, since you're reading this book BEFORE you take the test (hopefully!), I caught you just in the nick of time, and there are a few **Magic Nuggets** that I want to pass along to you to help you prepare. Consider this the dessert.

First of all, get yourself a good study guide. I have a favorite study guide that I use with all of my students, but since I don't know when you are reading this book, I don't know which ones will be available to you. **Magic Nugget** number one is pick one that explains the subject material well, especially the Math, and has good, readable explanations of the answers to the practice test questions. You can buy the guide or check it out at the library. I would encourage you to buy it, because then you can write in it all that you want. It should be treated as a work book, not a work of art.

I won't tell you to disregard what they say about test-taking techniques, because a few of the tips in these study guides are worthwhile. However, their test-taking tips tend to be shallow and dated. Take them with a grain of salt, and see if they line up with the techniques described in this book or more like the restrictor plate, "How I Take Tests."

Magic Nugget number two is <u>when you study, find a place that is free of distractions</u> (as much as possible). That means no television on, no music playing, no dog or cat licking on your face, and no boyfriend or girlfriend kissing on your ear! Oh no, I can hear the cries now, "But I like my television on/music playing/dog or cat licking/boyfriend or girlfriend kissing on me while I study!" Those are all great things, but they are detrimental to your learning. Remember, the conscious mind can only process one thing at a time, so if you interrupt that, you take your conscious mind out of use. The subconscious mind is taking in everything else, so background distractions are absorbed instead of useful information.

People, especially teenagers, like to think of themselves as "multitaskers," but multitasking promotes easily distracted brains, rather than brains that focus. Studies have shown that rather than doing any one thing well, multitaskers do many things mediocre. They don't think they're doing them mediocre, because they compare themselves to other multitaskers. Simply put, multitasking impairs learning. Multitaskers deal superficially with information, thereby preventing any lasting memory of it.

The use of multiple senses (seeing, hearing, touching, smelling, and tasting) enhances the ability to remember things, so (**Magic Nugget**) use as many senses as possible when studying. The brain gets input from multiple sources, so each sense reinforces the memory making it stronger. Want to remember something? Write it down (touch), read it (sight), and say it out loud (hearing). If you use some kind of aromatic candle or air freshener while you study, smelling that same fragrance later will trigger the memory. Be creative. Burn a vanilla candle while studying, and then put a little vanilla extract under your chin before you go in to take the test.

Mild stress, like the kind encountered while taking a timed test, actually helps memory through the release of adrenalin. Repeated testing also enhances the memory of processes and procedures (like those used in the Math section), so (**Magic Nugget**) do a lot of practice testing in your preparation. Make sure, however, that any missed problems are reviewed to find the error and correct it. That's why a study guide with good test question explanations is so important. You don't want to reinforce poor judgment, wrong procedures, or bad habits, so redo the missed problem the correct way as soon after taking the test as possible. Get it into your brain the right way. Whoever said, "Practice makes perfect" was wrong. PERFECT practice makes perfect, so go back, and do it right!

Here's something to encourage you to study. It has been found that training your memory actually makes you feel good. A biological reward comes from the release of the neurotransmitter dopamine. The dopamine release is promoted by performing tasks, like studying and practice testing, that "exercise" your memory. Dopamine receptors mediate feelings of euphoria and reward, so "exercising" your memory gives you a "feel good" jolt.

The last **Magic Nugget** is to get plenty of sleep: 8 to 9 hours preferably. And I don't mean the night before the test, although that is good, too. I mean EVERY night. Why is sleep so important when you are trying to learn? Because the brain works during sleep. It takes the memories of the day, consolidates them, organizes them into a reasonable structure, and tucks them into bed in the storage recesses of your brain. Shortening or disrupting the sleep cycle short circuits this process. Simply put, sleep loss equals memory loss, so sleep well after studying and learning. It will cement in those memories rather than losing them, because the following night's sleep will only capture the memories of THAT day. You can catch up on lost sleep to help your body regenerate, but you can't catch up on lost memories.

Magic Nugget Review

1) Pick a good study guide that explains the subject material well, especially the Math, and has good, readable explanations of the answers to the practice test questions.

2) When you study, pick a place that is free of distractions.

3) Use as many senses (seeing, hearing, touching, feeling, and tasting) as possible when studying. The more senses used, the stronger the memory.

4) Do a lot of practice testing during your preparation, but remember to correct all missed questions as soon as possible. Remember, only PERFECT practice makes perfect.

5) Sleep loss means memory loss, so sleep well after every day of studying in addition to the night before the test. The preferred length is 8 to 9 hours.

Don't Be Afraid to Go Out on a Limb – That's Where the Fruit Is

In closing, let me say that you have been endowed by your creator with a magnificent tool: your mind. It is capable of all that is imaginable. Every great work of art, every majestic architectural marvel, every beautiful song, and every technological wonder was conceived in someone's mind first. But your mind will also never go beyond what you allow it to do. You have to free your mind from all doubt, fear, and disbelief. The only restrictions on your mind are those that you place on it yourself.

Take the help and advice presented on these pages and ACT on it! In the Bible, it says in James 2:17, "faith by itself, if it is not accompanied by action, is dead." So, too, is the advice in this book dead if you do not put it into action. Galatians 6:9 also says, "Let us not become weary in doing good, for at the proper time we will reap a harvest if we do not give up." Take this to heart, as well. DO NOT GIVE UP!

There is always a learning curve with any new skill and ability. The learning curve is short for some and longer for others, but THE CURVE ALWAYS TURNS UP if you stick with it and DO NOT GIVE UP.

Sometimes the toughest thing to do is the dirty work. You know what I'm talking about: studying and practicing when nobody's watching. That means spending hours in the library or your bedroom when you would rather be out with your friends. Well, here are a few thoughts about doing the dirty work. Muhammad Ali said, "I hated every minute of training, but I said, 'Don't quit. Suffer now and live the rest of your life as a champion'." "Start by doing what's necessary, then do what's possible, and suddenly you are doing the impossible." – Francis of Assisi.

On the day that you take the test, smile as you confidently stride into the room. Take a deep breath, and smell the sweet smell of success that you KNOW is coming your way, because you have prepared your car for this race. The restrictor plate has been removed, and you are about to unleash the FULL POWER of your conscious and subconscious minds working together in complete harmony and effectiveness.

110

Remember this day with pride as the day that propelled you full speed into a life of achievement and success.

Finally, there are many truisms in life. One of these is, "Life is like a ten-speed bicycle. Most of us have gears we never use." Promise yourself that you will always use all of your gears.

I wish you good luck and good testing!

Sources and Suggested Reading

1)   Amen, Daniel G. *Magnificent Mind At Any Age*. New York. Crown Publishing. 2008.

2)   Balf, Todd. "The story behind the SAT overhaul." *New York Times*. March 6, 2014.

3)   Grabmeier, Jeff. "SAT test prep tools give advantage to students from wealthier families." *Ohio State Research News*. August 6, 2006. http://researchnews.osu.edu/archive/satprep.htm.

4)   Klemm, W. R. *Memory Power 101: A Comprehensive Guide to Better Learning for Students, Businesspeople, and Seniors*. New York. Skyline Publishing. 2012.

5)   Montgomery, Paul and Jane Lilly. "Systematic reviews of the effects of preparatory courses on university entrance examinations in high school-age students." *International Journal of Social Welfare*. Volume 21, Issue 1, 3 – 12. January 2012.

6) Perelman, Les. Interview by Linda Wertheimer. PBS. May 7, 2005.

http://www.npr.org/templates/story/story.php?storyId=4634566

7) Robinson, Adam and John Katzman. *Cracking the SAT*. New York. Random House LLC. 2014.

8) Wake Forest University Baptist Medical Center. "Listen up, tune out: Training and experience can affect brain." News release. November 6, 2007.

Websites: http://www.act.org (ACT)

http://www.collegeboard.org (SAT)

49730539R00074